Tree

by Margie Burton, Cathy French, and Tammy Jones

Table of Contents

What Are the Parts of a Tree?

There are many kinds of trees.
Can you see some ways
that the trees are alike?

All trees have trunks.
All trees have branches.
All trees have leaves or needles.
All trees have roots.

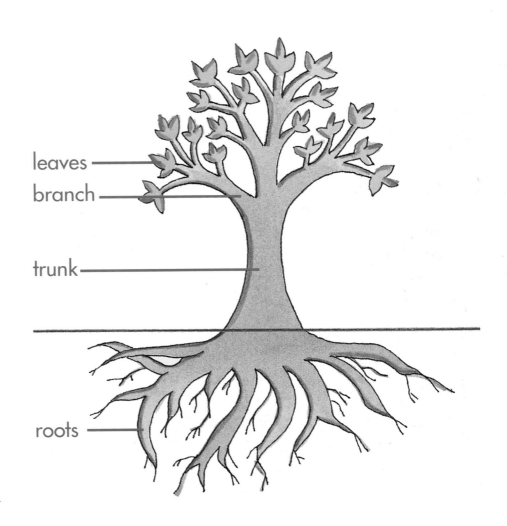

Trees have many shapes.
Some trees look like a circle.
Some trees look like a triangle.

All trees have trunks.
The trunk of a tree
gets bigger as it grows.

All trees have branches.
The branches grow from the trunk.

All trees have leaves or needles.
The leaves grow from the branches.
The tree gets its food from the leaves.
The leaves of all trees do not look alike.

How are these leaves different?

When Do Most Trees Lose Their Leaves?

Many trees lose their leaves in the fall. They grow new ones in the spring.

These are needles.
They stay green all the time.
When the needles fall off,
some new needles grow.

How Do Roots Help a Tree?

All trees have roots.
The roots help hold the tree
in the ground.

The water from the soil
goes into the roots to help
the tree grow.

Why Do Trees Have Seeds?

All trees have seeds.
They do not all look alike.
New trees grow from the seeds.

How Can Trees Help Animals?

Some animals use the seeds for food.

Some animals make their homes in the trunk of a tree.

Birds make their home on the branches of a tree.

How Can Trees Help People?

Trees can keep us cool.
It is much cooler to sit
in the shade of a tree
than it is to sit in the hot sun.

Many trees are cut down
for us to use. We use
the wood in our fireplace
so we can keep warm.

We use the wood
to make paper.

We also use the wood
from trees to build houses.

We also use trees for fun.

Would you like to plant a tree?
Here's how to do it.

1. Fill a cup with some
   soil.

2. Add water.

3. Place
   a tree seed
   in the soil.

4. Place a plastic
   bag on top of
   the cup.

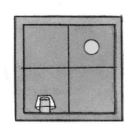 

5. Put the cup in
   a sunny, warm
   place.

6. Water the
   soil as needed
   to keep it damp.

Maybe your tree will look like this one day!